See Spot Sit

Carol Lea Benjamin

See Spot Sit

101 Illustrated Tips
for Training the Dog You Love

Skyhorse Publishing

www.skyhorsepublishing.com

Library of Congress Cataloging-in-Publication Data

Benjamin, Carol Lea.
See spot sit : 101 illustrated tips for training the dog you love /
Carol Lea Benjamin.
p. cm.
ISBN 978-1-60239-259-5 (pbk. : alk. paper)
1. Dogs--Training. I. Title.

SF431.B424 2008
636.7'0887--dc22
2007049528

10 9 8 7 6 5 4 3 2 1

Printed in China

Good friends are worth more than gold.

For Richard Siegel and Polly DeMille,
and for Sky who helped me write this book
by being a puppy at just the perfect time

Contents

1
How to Have a Happy Dog
1

2
Good Manners Last a Lifetime
27

3
The ABCs of Dog Training
49

4
Play It Safe
83

5
Good Times, Fun, and Games
95

1

How to Have a Happy Dog

1. **Planning ahead will save the day.** Your new pup will need a safe place to stay when you cannot watch him; a variety of chew toys; a simple collar and leash; wholesome food; pans for food and water; and a humane schedule for meals, playtime, and housetraining that will change as he grows up.

2. When you **find the perfect name** for your brand new pup, say it out loud twenty-five times. If you still love it, then it's the right name for your new best friend.

3. **Dogs need exercise,** outside, every single day, rain or shine.

How to Have a Happy Dog

4. **Every pup needs a den**, someplace where he can be safe when no one's able to watch him and a place he can go where he knows he won't be disturbed. The easiest way to provide a den is to use a puppy crate, available from pet-supply stores or catalogs. It should be large enough so that your puppy can lie down and stretch out comfortably, with some extra space for growth. I always leave something for my pup to chew on and drape her crate with a towel to make it cozier inside.

5. **Learn to understand your dog's body language** so that you know what he is "saying."

6. You may find it surprising to know that if you **speak "dog,"** your dog will understand you.

7. You can help your dog understand *your* language if you **teach one word at a time.**

8. Think positively. It works!

9. Teach your new puppy to walk up and down stairs by holding his leash taut, but not tight, to offer him support. Start him out in the middle of the flight so that he has no choice but to walk up or down. Praise him as he goes.

10. Be patient. It takes time to train a dog.

11. **Respect is a two-way street.** Don't encourage your dog to be a pest by responding to his every whim when you're busy. Your dog, too, will need time to eat, sleep, and daydream without being interrupted.

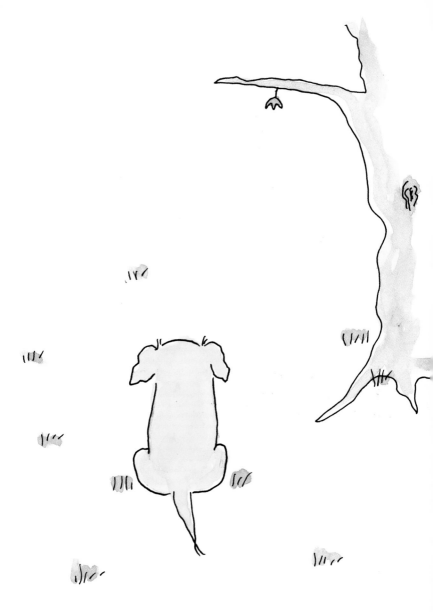

How to Have a Happy Dog

13

12. For a cat-friendly dog, **introduce your pup to a dog-friendly cat** and let them play about once a week.

13. In order to raise a dog you can take anywhere, **accustom your dog to walking on a variety of surfaces.**

14. In order to have a dog who's wonderfully blasé about new things, **make sure he gets around town and meets lots and lots of people.**

15. When your puppy gets wild and starts to nip, or you feel tense, take a hike. Time outside will make you both feel surprisingly mellow.

How to Have a Happy Dog

16. Dogs are smarter than most people think. No matter what size of dog you have, he needs challenges for his fabulous brain.

17. Help your dog use his energy in a constructive way, taking long walks, playing with other dogs, retrieving a ball, learning the basic commands, and playing lots of silly games. That way he'll have less energy for excessive barking, destructive chewing, stealing food, rummaging through the trash, and tossing toys at you while you are sleeping.

18. A calm owner helps create a calm dog. Baby talk, loud, squeaky noises, and constantly getting a dog worked up make for a frantic, nervous pet.

Instead, come and go without a fuss, expect your dog to spend some of his time contentedly gnawing on a bone or chew toy, and talk to your dog in a normal tone of voice.

How to Have a Happy Dog

19. Grooming time is bonding time. Make brushing your dog part of your relaxing, nighttime routine. Don't forget, dogs are the best listeners. They never interrupt and they never reveal your secrets.

20. If you **respond to your dog's attempts to communicate with you,** he will continue to try to tell you what he needs and what he's feeling. If you don't pay attention, you'll be missing some of the best conversations ever.

21. Dogs need balance in their lives: exercise, education, affection, company, fun, and games.

How to Have a Happy Dog

22. Overly modest goals lead to overly modest results. High expectations will help you and your best friend achieve the results you both deserve. So don't be afraid to dream big.

2

Good Manners Last a Lifetime

23. The simplest solution is usually the best one. When something gets your dog's attention in a bad way, making him bark and pull on his leash—a kid whizzing by on a skateboard, a jackhammer breaking up the street, a truck backing up (you never know what might bother a dog's sensitive hearing or what might catch his eye and inspire a chase)—get his attention onto you with a sound, a command, or by movement, speeding up your pace and calling him to keep up with you. Most dogs are not multi-taskers. They blissfully give all their attention to one thing at a time—that's one of the joys of being a dog and being with a dog. So replacing a "no, no" with a "yes, yes" will do the trick.

24. Think ahead. Don't let your dog do anything when he's little that you won't want him to do when he's all grown up.

25. Until your dog is trained, "prevention" should be your middle name. To stop your pup from tearing up the garbage, put the can under your kitchen sink behind closed doors. Temporarily keep your wastebasket on top of your desk (where mine is now). Prevent your dog from drinking out of the toilet by keeping your bathroom door closed or by closing the lid. Instead of kicking off your shoes, toss them in the closet and close the door. Your pup will assume that anything lying around on the floor and anything within reach belongs to him, so while he is still learning to play with his things and not yours, don't leave anything within his reach that might harm him—a glass of wine, cigarettes or matches, chocolate, medication, anything sharp. Also, be careful with anything you'd hate to lose.

See Spot Sit

26. If you **follow your puppy around the house**, you'll have the perfect opportunity to monitor his behavior, letting him know what he can chew on and what he must leave alone. A soft "good dog" or "no, leave it," will let him know which is which.

Good Manners Last a Lifetime

27. **A woof at the door is a good thing. A racket isn't.** When your dog begins to respond to the doorbell or a knock with a bark, tell him, "Good dog." That will make him look at you. Once you have his attention, tell him, "enough," letting him know you got the message and it doesn't bear repeating. In this way, you can teach your dog to alert you when someone's at the door, but not go ballistic every time a friend drops by or a pizza is delivered.

28. When your pup is naughty, don't take it personally. He hasn't grown up yet. He hasn't yet learned your house rules. Most importantly, he's still your best friend. He doesn't do bad things because he's spiteful or because he doesn't love you. He does them because he's a little dog in need of education. It takes a few months of training for him to learn what's okay to do and what isn't. So when he has an accident on the rug, take him out and show him *again* where he's supposed to go. And when you find him chewing something of yours, tell him "no," replace it with something of his, and tell him he's the best puppy ever born. He'll catch on.

29. Puppies will try to chew on anything and everything, even *you*. It's normal for puppies to explore the world with their mouths. Still, you should *never* let your puppy bite you, even in play. When he does—and he will—or when he nips at your pants as you walk by, tell him, "no," immediately give him something he *can* chew on, and praise him when he does.

See Spot Sit

30. What should you do when your pup is too wired up or too over tired to stop biting? What do you do when your little darling seems more like an alligator than a baby dog? Simple. When offering your puppy an alternative won't do the trick, that's your signal to take him out to relieve himself and then put him in his crate to let him chill out. Most likely, he'll go right to sleep and wake up his sweet old self.

31. House-train your puppy with the judicious use of a crate. Your pup's crate will not only keep him safe when there's no one available to watch him, but using a crate and a humane, practical schedule is also the best way to teach your puppy to relieve himself outside instead of all over your house.

When your pup is too young to have any control at all (around seven or eight weeks old), block off an area around the crate and make him a "yard" out of newspaper. Leave the crate door open so that he has a clean place to sleep, plus access to his "yard." Cleaning up frequently will help your puppy learn to keep clean indoors. At this age, puppies need to relieve themselves every twenty to thirty minutes when they are active. So if you are playing with your puppy indoors, make sure to get him out or to his papers that often.

At nine or ten weeks, you will be able to put your puppy on a schedule, crating him overnight and taking him for walks frequently during the day. As he grows up, he will be able to stay out of the crate for longer periods, as long as he is supervised.

7AM   Puppy out for a walk
Feed, kiss, play, train, walk
again

7³⁰   Crate puppy

10   Puppy out
Play, play, play, walk again

10³⁰   Crate puppy

12⁰⁰   Puppy out
Feed, play, kiss, kiss, kiss
walk again

Continue as above until
your bedtime.

32. **Dogs don't outgrow bad habits any more than people do.** They need to be *taught* not to nip, chew on our possessions, and relieve themselves indoors; this takes patience, time, and repetition. But even though it takes work and time to teach your pup some basic good manners, it takes even more work and more time to correct bad habits once they become an established part of your puppy's repertoire. Remember—"prevention" is your middle name.

33. Give housetraining a "name." Using a command helps your dog understand what he's supposed to do and where he's supposed to do it. You never know when you and your pup will find yourselves in a different environment—a train station, an airport, a city street with no grass. Having a word that lets your dog know that this is the place to relieve himself can save the day. You might tell him, "Hurry up," or "Go, go, go." Be sure to choose a command that won't be *too* embarrassing should someone overhear you.

A command for housetraining can be useful even when you're at home. It's a way to help paper-trained dogs learn to use the great outdoors. And on cold, dark, rainy nights when your dog needs one last walk and all you want to do is curl up under the covers and read a good book, you'll have a way of speeding up the process.

34. Give your dog appropriate greeting behavior. Like a lot of people, I'm a sucker for a cute little dog jumping up on me to say hello. But not every pup stays small. And not every human likes to be jumped on by a dog, especially one with muddy paws. So teach your dog a replacement behavior. Ask him to sit right before he's going to greet someone. You can even teach him to sit and give his paw. (See Tip 78.) That way, he can have the happy social experience of meeting friends and friendly strangers without getting you in trouble.

Good Manners Last a Lifetime

35. Even a grown dog needs a room of his own. Once your dog has bulletproof manners—he relieves himself out of doors and no longer tries to chew on your things—you can leave his crate open or even remove the door. Even trained, he will continue to love and use his den as a place to take a break when he needs it.

36. Want to have your cake and eat it too? If you teach the command "Leave it" (using a serious and deep—but not loud—voice), you can prevent your dog from eating your cake when you go to the kitchen to get your coffee.

37. Put jumping up on command. Once your dog learns a polite way to greet people, teach him to jump up on command. There's nothing easier. Simply pat your chest and tell your pup, "Up." Now his default setting will be to sit and greet, but anyone desiring more enthusiasm can override it with a command and praise.

Good Manners Last a Lifetime

38. **Teach your dog to go to his bed.** Suppose you want your dog in the room, but not all over you. You might be eating dinner, talking on the phone, bouncing a baby on your knee, or writing a book. There's no law that says your dog can have only one bed. So if there's one in your bedroom, put another in the living room. Teach him to go there and lie down by telling him to "Go to your bed," running there with him, and praising like mad when you get there. To make sure he's happy there while you are busy doing something else, give him a favorite bone or toy to chew.

39. When you begin to **teach your pup to stay alone**, tire him out before you leave. Take him for a long walk, practice his commands, play a fun game or two, and leave the radio playing when you go out so that the house sounds more like it does when you're at home. Don't stay away too long the first few times you leave him, and be warm but calm when you return.

40. Never laugh at your dog when he does something naughty, even if it's cute. Laughing tells him, "That was fun. Do it again."

3

The ABCs of Dog Training

41. All dogs need training.

42. *B*ad behavior can end a relationship.

43. *C*ommunication augments the loving bond between you and your dog.

44. Dogs need to know what's expected of them. Clear, simple training and a few easy-to-follow rules and routines make a dog feel secure.

45. Whisper, don't shout. Your dog's hearing is much keener than yours.

46. Your most important training tools cannot be purchased. They **are voice, posture, and attitude.** Dogs are pack animals. They need to have a kind, smart leader (that would be you!) in order to feel secure. Leadership will not only help your dog feel calm and safe, it will also make training easier.

Leadership is not about following a bunch of rules, and it's surely not about being mean to your dog. It means that you are confident and comfortable about teaching your dog and keeping him out of harm's way. Keeping your dog safe is the most important reason for training him.

As for equipment you *can* buy, a four- or six-foot leash and a plain buckle or snap collar are all you will need to train your puppy. Some equipment promises to do the work for you; but if something sounds too good to be true, it probably is. There is no "magic pill." It will take work and time to educate your dog and help him become the companion you dream of and deserve.

The ABCs of Dog Training

47. Teach your dog "No" and "Okay." "No" means "Don't do that." "Okay" means "Do whatever you want." Both are essential teaching tools and both can be taught by tone of voice.

48. Praise is the key to gentle and effective dog training. Warm and unobtrusive praise tells your dog you approve of what he's doing—so always praise him with kind words and a loving pat when he's doing something you want him to repeat, and never when he's being inappropriate.

49. **Dogs learn by repetition.** This doesn't mean you should repeat a command over and over again. It means you have to show your dog what you want a number of times and in a variety of places until he gets it. Some dogs need more repetition than others. No matter how quickly or slowly your dog learns, he *will* learn if you are patient, clear, and generous with your praise every time he gets it right.

The ABCs of Dog Training

50. Teach your dog to sit and stay on command. The *sit stay* is the easiest way to teach him how to pay attention, listen to words, and learn. Hold a toy over his head. When he has to look up, he will sit. Signal him to stay with an open hand, the same way you'd tell a person to stay or wait. Wait two seconds, then tell him "Okay" and praise him.

See Spot Sit

51. A correction tells your dog you don't approve of what he's doing, so correct him when he's doing something you don't want him to repeat. The mildest correction that works is always the one to use. For most goofs, just saying "no"—and meaning it— will get your message across.

52. It takes at least five different experiences in order for a dog to generalize. Start training your dog indoors. Once he gets the new command, try it outdoors. Next, work with him on a busy street, then where kids are running around, and finally where there are other dogs in view.

The ABCs of Dog Training

53. What if your puppy won't come when you call him? A reliable response to "Come!" is one habit you *must* establish. So if your pup decides not to come, try these tricks.

Make yourself smaller. Crouch down, throw your arms wide, and call in a sweet voice.

Make yourself irresistible. Call your pup and jingle your keys, squeeze a squeak toy, or show him his favorite ball. When he comes, toss the toy and let him catch or retrieve it.

Make yourself seem to disappear. Call your dog and run in the opposite direction. Everyone wants something he can't have. At the last minute, turn, crouch, and let him jump on you for kisses.

54. **For a reliable, speedy recall, ask a friend or two to help.** Sit opposite each other; or, if you have a few helpers, sit in a big circle and take turns calling your pup to come, kissing and praising him when he does. To speed up his recall, use squeak toys as lures, and hold your arms out wide to encourage him.

The ABCs of Dog Training

55. Teach your dog to look to you for direction. Ask him to sit. Hold a favorite toy and tell him, "Watch me." Move the toy slowly toward the side of your face until your pup is looking into your eyes. Praise him and give him the toy. Practice until he looks into your eyes whenever you say, "Watch me." Soon he will look into your eyes when he wants to know whether to turn the corner or keep going straight; when he wants to know if he's been naughty or nice; or simply when he wants to show you that he loves you.

56. Train your dog after you exercise him and before he eats. That way, he won't have ants in his pants, and he won't be so full that he'll need a nap instead of a lesson.

The ABCs of Dog Training

57. Attitude is everything. If you know you are humanely in charge, your dog will know that, too.

58. One success leads to another. If you end each and every training session with something your dog does well, something that makes him proud of himself, you will both look forward to the next day's training and start each new lesson with a can-do attitude.

59. Teach your dog to walk at your side. Walking on a leash shouldn't be a tug of war. If your dog pulls ahead, turn and walk in the opposite direction. If he lags behind, crouch and call him to you, arms held open for him. Or call him and run backward, turning at the last minute to let him catch you. Always praise him warmly when he stays calm and close.

The ABCs of Dog Training

60. Some dogs react best to voice signals, some to whistles, some to hand signals. As you train your dog, try different ways of signaling him. When you find the one he responds to best, use it as your main form of communication.

The ABCs of Dog Training

61. Teach your dog the "down" command when he's really tired. Cheating? No, smart. Pat the floor, tell him, "Down," and stretch out the word so that it sounds like "dooown." Or ask him to sit and lure him down with his favorite toy. Practice after he exercises every day.

62. When you are going to teach something new, start with something old. In this way, starting with a nifty *sit stay* (see Tip 50) or a cheery recall (see Tip 54), you will get your dog's attention and let him know that he's about to do some interesting work. When you finish working on the new command (three or four repetitions at one time are enough), give the dog a command he knows well and end the lesson with lots of praise.

63. When you are teaching something new and your dog gets it on his own for the first time, don't ask him to do it again. Instead, praise him like crazy, end the session, and play his favorite game.

64. **Dogs pattern-train quickly.** You can use this to your advantage by requesting that your dog sit at the door while you put on his collar and leash before a walk, before you put his food bowl down, and when greeting a friend or a friendly stranger.

65. Once your dog knows a command—"sit," "come," "leave it," or "lie down"—integrate it into your everyday life with him. Once you can use a command, you don't have to practice it any longer. Using it will be his practice. If you have no use for any particular command, don't bother to teach it in the first place.

66. Vary the time of your training sessions from very short (a minute or two) to moderate (ten minutes). Once your dog has learned several commands and does them reliably, occasionally work with him for twenty minutes or more at a time, interspersing some fast walking with commands that keep him still and let him think—such as a *sit stay* or "lie down."

67. *Sit down* is not a command. "Sit" is one command. "Down" is another. Sometimes success is just a matter of clarity.

68. Mix up the order of your training. Don't let your dog predict your lesson plan—it will encourage him to daydream. Instead, keep him sharp by changing your routine so that he has to listen to your words and watch for your hand signals in order to get it right.

69. The very best reward you can give your dog is your pleasure. If you reward your dog with food, he will look at your hands, or worse, your pockets. If you reward your dog with praise and petting, he will look into your eyes.

70. Training sessions should be fun for you and your dog. Work in little bursts that will resemble the way you'll use the commands once they are integrated into your life with your dog. Do a "sit" here, a recall there, a quick "lie down," and then a game of fetch. You'll be surprised how much your dog can learn in just a few minutes, and how much he can learn while you are both playing and having a great time.

The ABCs of Dog Training

71. Keep your sense of humor. You'll need it.

4

Play It Safe

72. Correct any and all signs of aggression. A serious "no" usually does the trick. If your dog is still nipping at your clothes or biting your hands, stop playing with him and give him some time in his crate to chill out. Fifteen or twenty minutes is usually enough time for the attitude adjustment you're after.

73. Never break your dog's command when you see he's going to break it without waiting for you to release him. If your dog gets to decide when to walk away from a *sit stay* or whether or not to come when you call him, he's surely smart enough to figure out that he's in charge. It's up to you, not him, to release your dog with a cheerful "Okay" and praise. So when your dog starts to get up from his *sit stay*, or if he finds something more important to do before coming when you call him, tell him "no" and repeat the command. When he tests his limits, you have the perfect opportunity to tighten his training, showing him once again what it is you want him to do. Remember that the right command, issued in a timely manner, can save your dog's life. His safety and your sanity depend on his *reliable* obedience to a few basic commands.

Play It Safe

74. Let sleeping dogs lie, but not on your bed or sofa. Sharing sleeping and sitting surfaces makes dogs feel they are your equal and that they should be running the show. Unless your dog is absolutely unaggressive and until he is reasonably obedient, let him sleep in his own bed, not yours.

75. Don't carry your little dog unless danger's afoot. It can make him feel unsure of himself, and insecurity can lead to aggression.

grrr

76. Don't carry your big dog. It's bad for your back.

77. Never pat a dog when he's acting aggressively. Patting won't calm him down. It will tell him that he's doing exactly what you want him to do. If you are outside with him, tell him "no" and then get him moving. Do not give him the chance to obsess over whatever is making him growl or bark. If he acts aggressively when you're at home, see Tip 72.

78. Teach your dog to shake "hands" on command. Since pawing is a submissive (friendly) gesture, the classic "give your paw" trick reminds your dog to be friendly to humans each time he slaps his paw into someone's hand.

See Spot Sit

79. Don't bother your dog when he's eating. If you absolutely need him when he's in the middle of a meal, don't reach out and touch him. Call him instead. This is an especially good rule to teach to children.

80. Play actively, not aggressively. Toss a ball, have a race, share a swim, take a hike to the dog park, and give your dog a chance to run and play with other dogs. Do not let your dog bite your arm in play. You never want your dog to think it's okay to bite you or any other human.

81. Always make your dog glad to come when you call. Coming when called cannot be viewed as an option. So never call your dog to come when he's made a mistake or you have to do something he might not like—i.e., cleaning his ears or cutting his nails. Doing that could teach him to run the other way when you call. In those cases, go and get him. *Do* call your dog for dinner, for a walk, for a game of fetch. And praise him extensively when he gets to you. That will make him happy to come whenever you call.

82. **Don't give your dog more freedom than he can handle.** Until he learns to relieve himself outside and not chew your possessions, do not give him run of the house unless you are following him around to monitor his behavior and make sure he and your possessions are safe.

83. When your dog hits adolescence, go back to square one. Is your dog around eight months of age? Has everything you've ever taught him gone down the drain? Relax. It's normal. Remember your adolescence? Simply go over all his training, reminding him often of the words he must obey and the rules he has to follow. Not to worry. He'll grow up. You did.

84. Behind almost every dog problem is the dog's need for more exercise. A tired dog is a good dog. A very tired dog is a *very* good dog.

5

Good Times, Fun, and Games

85. Hang out with your puppy. The time you spend with him early on—training, playing, watching, and learning—will pay you back more than you might imagine.

Good Times, Fun, and Games

86. Give your dog active time every single day, thereby constantly allowing him the chance to use his mind, his muscles, his fabulous ability to find things by their scent. Being able to work and be outside will help your dog feel relaxed, satisfied, and calm.

Good Times, Fun, and Games

87. Give your dog quiet time. Dogs are contemplative creatures. They need time to process what they have learned and time to just chill out when they feel stressed or tired.

One minute later...

88. **Routine is good.** It offers your dog the comfort of knowing what's expected of him and the pleasure of anticipating what comes next, like the game you play with him at the end of each training session.

Good Times, Fun, and Games

89. Surprise is good. Change your dog's routine. Take him to the park for training and a run with his buddies; feed him out of doors; run away and call him to come and catch you; give him an empty water bottle to crunch and carry on a walk. Surprise keeps your dog alert.

Good Times, Fun, and Games

90. If you toss a ball down your hallway, there's a pretty good chance your dog will chase it and bring it back to you. Praise him and toss the ball again. Keep the game light, informal, and fun. Once your dog enjoys fetching a ball, you can toss one as a reward when you are teaching him the things he needs to know.

91. Throw the ball far, but not high. Dogs can get injured if they jump too high.

92. Work and play like a pro. Professional train-
ers never miss the opportunity to teach. You can
do the same thing. It doesn't take any more time than you
are already spending with your dog. It doesn't spoil the
fun either. In fact, it adds to the revelry. When your dog
brings you a toy, hoping to entice you into a game, name
the toy. Toss him the duck, the pig, or the ball, just as
always, but tell him, "Take the duck." Then, "Bring the
duck." You'll be increasing your dog's vocabulary while
you play. Some dogs can boast (if dogs boasted) vocabular-
ies of over 100 words. Name all the toys; name all the
activities; praise your dog for getting it right.

93. Choose games and tricks that your dog does or can do naturally. Watch your dog at play. Does he love to bark? Teach him "Speak, count, add" (see Tip 94). Is he light on his feet, born to jump? Teach him to jump over your leg, over a stick, or through a hoop. Is he a hound with big floppy ears who seems to live in his nose? All dogs love scent games. Hounds love them best. Is your dog sleepy and close to the ground? Does he snore? Playing dead is his trick of choice. "Roll over" is another, if you're ambitious. There's a trick for every dog, and finding the ones that are best suited to your dog's body type and personality is the best trick of all.

94. Speak, count, add. Your dog barks when someone knocks on the door, doesn't he? Barking at the door is natural for most dogs, usually starting at adolescence (about six months or older). Once he starts, he will bark to announce the mailman, visitors, the meter reader. You can wait for those events, or better still, ask a friend to stop by and ring your bell or knock on the door. Tell your about-to-bark dog, "Speak, good dog, speak," and you are well on your way. Practice when the occasion presents itself, for once your dog will bark on command, the trick to stopping him is praise. Praise will get him to stop barking and look at you. Praise again for his attention.

Next, switch the verbal command "Speak" to a hand signal. Pointing at the dog will do. Say, "Speak," and point. After a week, your dog will bark when you point a finger at him. Now you can ask your dog to count to five as you point at him. (If he doesn't get it, coax him along by saying, "Come on. *Speak* up.") Once he's barked five times, praise him so that he stops. Now ask him, "How much is two and two?" as you point. When he's barked four times, tell him he's the world's smartest dog, because, of course, he is. Your friends will think that you're a genius, too, and they're probably right.

Good Times, Fun, and Games

95. Paws up. Like "Speak," "Paws up" can be the foundation work for several tricks. It's taught by tapping an elevated surface as you encourage your dog to put his paws there by saying, "Paws up, good dog." Start by sitting and tapping your knees. "Paws up. Good dog." Your dog will want to get close enough for a pat and a kiss. If you are cheerful and encouraging, he should learn this in no time.

96. **Close the door.** This silly trick can be useful, too. Once your dog knows "Paws up" and you have practiced it on your knees, the kitchen counter, and the edge of your bed (and praised him warmly), open a door just a few inches, tapping it as you tell him, "Paws up, close the door." As he gets better and better at the task, you will be able to open the door a little wider and signal him to close it by putting his paws on it. Some dogs love this trick and the louder the door slams, the more they like it. Sound-sensitive dogs will not like this trick; but if you have one of those, not to worry. There's more to come.

Good Times, Fun, and Games

97. Find the biscuit. This game is a winner because it gives your dog the chance to use his extraordinary sense of smell, and, at the same time, reinforce his ability to hold the "stay" command. Once your dog knows his *sit stay*, ask him to sit and stay and briefly let him smell a small piece of dog biscuit. (If he tries to eat it, tell him, "Smell it," as you close your hand.) Now, reminding him once more to stay, place the biscuit a foot or two in front of him, wait no more than three seconds, and tell him, "Find it." He will, and he'll eat it, too. So far, so good. You can repeat Step One several times daily for a week.

Each week, place the biscuit a little farther away and have your dog wait a little longer. After a few weeks, if your dog is doing well, place the biscuit in the next room but in such an obvious place that he'll see it as soon as he gets to the doorway. Once your dog is actually using his nose to find the biscuit (you will actually hear him sniffing), you can ask him to find a favorite toy. Always have him smell the object first. Always name it as well. At any time, if your dog cannot find the object, it merely means you've gone too fast. Just go back and try again, making it easier. In dog training, going slowly is faster than going fast. Your most important job is to help your dog succeed.

Good Times, Fun, and Games

98. **Jump over a stick.** Start with a stick or a broom. Lay it right down on the floor. Walk your dog over it, telling him, "Over." After your dog is used to the stick lying on the ground, prop it up on two bricks or shoeboxes and continue. Always take the "jump" with your dog and encourage him in a cheerful voice. After a few weeks, you will be able to send your dog over the stick by tossing a ball over it, making sure that there's no way to go around it. Then call him back, saying, "Over." What else can your dog jump over? Now there's nothing between you and David Letterman's "Stupid Pet Tricks" but your imagination.

Roll over!

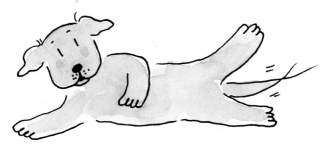

99. **Roll over.** This trick requires patience, but once learned, dogs love doing it. When your dog responds well to "Down," ever so gently roll him over, giving him the command. Once your dog is relaxed about rolling over, start to cue him by making a circle with your hand. This classic trick is really cute and should earn you and your dog a hearty round of applause.

100. Catch two ways. The easiest way to teach your dog to catch is to ask him to sit and stay and then toss a small piece of food for him. He probably won't catch it the first few times. You can let him find it and eat it anyway. But once he starts to catch the treat, the rules change. Now, in order to eat the treat, he must catch it. After a week of catching small bits of biscuit, try your dog with a small toy or soft ball, telling him to catch it and praising him when he does. Most dogs love this game and will bring you toys to toss for them.

Once your dog is hooked on catching things, try getting him to catch a ball off a bounce. Again, like the first time, it might take him a few days to catch on. But he'll get it—and soon enough he'll know which way the ball is coming by the way you position your hand right before you toss.

Good Times, Fun, and Games

101. **Wave goodbye.** After you teach your dog to give his paw, hold out your hand as you would to accept his paw. As he lifts his paw, turn your hand over and lift it about a foot, saying, "Wave goodbye." Your dog will lift his paw to try to get it into yours, moving it around to reach your hand as if he's waving goodbye. This is an adorable trick and the perfect ending for a visit from friends—or a book of tips on how to train your dog.

Don't forget, dogs live in the moment. Playing games with your dog is one of the best ways to live in the moment with him. It might just turn out to be the most satisfying part of your day.